Singh

by Iain Gray

PUBLISHING

WRITING *to* REMEMBER

79 Main Street, Newtongrange,
Midlothian EH22 4NA
Tel: 0131 344 0414   Fax: 0845 075 6085
E-mail: info@lang-syne.co.uk
www.langsyneshop.co.uk

Design by Dorothy Meikle
Printed by Blissetts
© Lang Syne Publishers Ltd 2021

All rights reserved. No part of this publication may be reproduced, stored or introduced into a retrieval system, or transmitted in any form or by any means (electronic, mechanical, photocopying, recording or otherwise) without the prior written permission of Lang Syne Publishers Ltd.

ISBN 978-1-85217-341-8

Chapter one:
Origins of names from the Indian subcontinent

by Iain Gray

With a population of more than one billion souls, India is the second most populated country in the world, while Pakistan, with more than 182 million, is ranked sixth and Bangladesh fifth.

Part of the vast Indian subcontinent, India is a nation that is home to a rich mix of ethnic groups, religions and cultures – and this is reflected on a truly dramatic scale through the immense variety of family names and naming conventions.

These are names found today not only in India itself, but also scattered throughout the world as many Indians, in common with the Scots and the Irish of earlier generations, sought fresh opportunities for themselves and their kinsfolk in foreign lands.

This, in turn, has not only added to the cultural diversity of those nations in which they settled and in which their descendants now thrive, but has also seen the importation to the West of what were previously wholly 'foreign' names.

These are commonly found in telephone directories throughout the world today, but to trace their origins we have to travel back through the dim mists of time to the great sub-continent of India itself – a vast landmass which from earliest times was home to a highly sophisticated civilisation.

The naming conventions and styles are as complex – often bewilderingly so – as they are varied, with significant differences occurring.

These are not only among the nation's states, or regions, such as Gujarat, West Bengal, Bihar, Jharkhand, Orissa, Andhra Pradesh, Himachal Pradesh, Rajasthan, Uttarakhand, Uttar Pradesh, Delhi, Manipur, Maharashtra, Chhattisgarh, Jammu and Kashmir, Goa and Haryana, for example, but also within the regions themselves.

Large concentrations of certain names are found within particular regions – but, it should be stressed, not all are solely confined to only one region.

Karavadra, *Lal*, *Patel* and *Shah* are common in Gujarat, where the language is Gujarati.

Names such as *Baidya*, *Chatterjee* and *Gupta* are found in West Bengal, where the language is

Bengali, while in the Hindi-speaking regions of Bihar and Jharkhand commonly found names include *Akhauri, Dhanjit, Pathik, Singh* and *Sinha*.

In Orissa, where the language is Oriya, names such as *Patnaik, Hati, Raj, Guru, Padhi, Samantray* and, again, *Singh*, predominate, while in the Telugu-speaking region of Andhra Pradesh common last names include *Adhikaria, Badam, Chowdary, Dasari, Godavarthi, Naidu, Setty* and *Varma*.

In the areas of Himachal Pradesh, Rajasthan, Uttarakhand, Uttar Pradesh and Delhi, where a number of different languages are spoken, popular names include *Agrawal, Bhati, Chand, Chaudhary, Dhowi, Khatri, Mathur, Panwar, Rana, Shahalia, Verma* and *Vajpai*.

In the Manipuri-speaking region of Manipur, frequently found names include those of *Yumnan, Konsam, Sewram, Chakpram, Kam* and *Oinam*, while in the Marathi-speaking area of Maharashtra commonly found names include *Mojad, Sarud, Soman, Pandit, Rasam* and *Sutar*.

In Chhattisgarh, where the languages spoken are Hindi and Chattisgarhi, names include *Agharia, Bhoi, Chandrakar, Nishad* and *Sahu*, while in Jammu and Kashmir, where the languages are

Kashmiri and Dogri, frequently found names include those of *Bhat*, *Maam*, *Rajwal*, *Sahgal*, *Samyal*, *Sharma* and *Tiku*.

Those found in Goa, where the languages are both Konkani and Marathi, include *Khandeparkar*, *Mendes*, *Parikar*, *Prabhu* and *Vernekar*, while in the Hindi and Haryanvi-speaking region of Haryana, common names include *Ahlawat*, *Beniwal*, *Dahiya*, *Saini* and *Talwar*.

Over the centuries many diverse factors have influenced the choice and the development of Indian family names – the key ones being not only those of language, or dialect, but those of ancestral birthplace, occupation, caste and religion.

In the majority of cases, but by no means exclusively, children are given three names – those of a 'given' one that roughly corresponds to the convention in the West of giving a child a 'Christian' forename, a second name, and a family, or third, one.

In some areas, where family names are not used, the third name may take the form of a revered religious figure or that of a grandfather or grandmother.

For those Hindus who belong to the upper

castes, their ancestry is indicated through what is known as his or her *gotra* – normally the name of an ancestor on the father's side, although it could also indicate the name of the ancestral village or profession.

Also in Hindu names, the family name frequently denotes the particular caste or community of Hindus to which the person belongs.

It is also common for Hindu families to hold a special name-giving ceremony shortly after a child's birth – after a horoscope of the child has been drawn up.

Adding further colour to the Hindu naming process is that many young children are also bestowed with a nickname – one chosen by either a family member or a close friend of the family.

In the religious community of the Sikhs, the majority of first names stem from ones derived from the classical language known as Sanskrit.

Sikh boys are also required to take the name of 'Singh' as a middle name, followed by a surname, or family name – while females of the faith are given the middle name of 'Kaur' or 'Gaur'.

Those Indians of the Jain faith frequently use 'Jain' as their last name, while many Jains of the

Gujarati region also use 'Shah' – derived from the Sanskrit word *sadhu*, denoting a monk.

Those Indians of the Muslim faith use Arabic names as their first, middle and last names.

Some, however, also use Indian names, particularly ones from the Urdu language – but only on strict condition that these names are not identified with any other religion.

The use of initials or abbreviations, rather than the full name, is very common with Indian names – the Punjabi cricketer Vikram Raj Vir Singh, more commonly known as V.R.V. Singh, being just one of many examples.

Adding to the rich variety of Indian names are those that derive from a particular occupation or profession.

One notable example is that of the great Indian social reformer, moral teacher and patriot Mohandas Karamchand Gandhi, better known to posterity as Mahatma Gandhi – whose family belonged to the caste of 'Gandhis', or 'grocers'.

The surnames of many Parsis, meanwhile, often end with 'wala', or 'wallah', indicating their line of work – such as 'Cyclewala', denoting a seller of bicycles.

Even more colourfully in recent years has been the practice of some Indians to adopt as their surname the English word for a particular profession – such as 'Engineer' – while, as in the West, it is also increasingly common to name children after famous celebrities such as film and sports stars.

But what all bearers of names have – be they of Indian, English, Scottish, Irish, Welsh or any other roots, and no matter where they are settled – is an ancient and indissoluble link with the country in which the name originated, making them heirs to its proud heritage and traditions.

Chapter two:

The Pure Ones

A name that resonates throughout the vibrant drama that is India's long history, 'Singh' is a Hindi word derived from the Sanskrit *simha*, meaning 'lion.'

This is a fitting title for a clan that was royal and warrior-like and which for centuries was at the very heart of India's frequently turbulent affairs. But the name is also found today in many other countries.

In the United Kingdom, for example, with close on 125,000 Singhs, it is ranked as the 379th most common; with nearly 1,700 bearers in the Greater Glasgow area, it is the 226th most popular, while it is the 60th most common in the Scottish Borders.

Also in Scotland, a Singh tartan is officially registered with the Scottish Register of Tartans.

In London, where there are more than 8,000 bearers, it is ranked 49th.

Adopted as a baptismal name by adherents of the Sikh faith at the close of the seventeenth century, it had been borne for several centuries previously by the Hindu Rajput warriors.

Its Punjabi form is 'Singh', while its Gujarati form is 'Sinh', and in the Sikh baptism ceremony known as *Khande di Pahul*, or *Amrit Sanchar*, boys are given the name 'Singh', meaning 'strong as a lion', or 'great warrior', while females are bestowed with 'Kaur', or 'Gaur', meaning 'princess.'

Originally a hereditary title, rather than a name, it is now commonly used by Sikhs as a middle name, although some use it as a last name in place of that of the 'clan' or 'family.'

This is illustrated in *Chapter four*, where the lives and times of some famous bearers of the name, both past and present, are featured.

Whether as a middle name or a surname, it is estimated that approximately 20 million adherents of the Khalsa, Kshatriya and Rajput Sikh faiths throughout the world use it today.

To find out how Sikhs came to adopt the name of Singh, we have to travel back through time to one of the most revered figures of the Sikh faith – Guru Gobind Singh, the 10th and last living Guru of Sikhism.

The impact on the Sikh faith of this philosopher, poet, warrior and founder and first commander-in-chief of the Sikh Khalsa Army cannot be overestimated.

He was the last in a line of living Gurus that began with Guru Nanak Dev ji, the founder of Sikhism, who was born into a Hindu family in the village of Talwandi – now present day Nankana Sahib – near Lahore.

He died in 1538, and was followed in succession as Guru by Guru Angad Dev ji, Guru Amardas ji, Guru Ramdas ji, Guru Arjan Dev ji, Guru Hargobind Dev ji, Guru Har Rai Dev ji, Guru Harkrishan Dev ji, Guru Tegh Bahadur ji and, finally, the great Guru Gobind Singh ji.

The dramatic and inspiring life and times of this Guru embrace not only some of the most important episodes in the history of the Sikh faith in particular, but also India's colourful history in general.

Born on December 22, 1666, in Patna, Bihar, he became Guru, or leader of the Sikh faith, at the age of nine, succeeding his father Guru Tegh Bahadur ji.

Born as Gobind Rai, there is an enduring legend that his birth had been foretold by a fakir known as Pir Bhikan Shah.

It is said that on one occasion Bhikan Shah bowed towards the east during his prayers, which was contrary to his normal Islamic practice of bowing in the direction of Mecca.

Questioned on this, he prophesied that a special child would be born in Patna, which lay to the East.

Bhikan Shah then set out on the long and dusty trail to Patna with a group of his followers to see this wondrous child.

Arriving at his humble home, he placed two bowls of sweets before the infant – one of the bowls having been bought from the shop of a Hindu and one from the shop of a Muslim.

The child placed his hands on both the bowls – indicating, according to legend, that both Muslims and Hindus would be treated equally by him.

Another legend holds that the fakir Araf Din, of Lakhnaur, which is now in Ambala District, also bowed before the boy and proclaimed him 'divine'.

Trained in military skills and horse riding by a Rajput warrior, he was formally installed as Guru on November 11, 1675 and went on to fight twenty defensive battles against the Mughals and their allies after inculcating martial skills among his army of devoted followers.

In early 1699 he sent letters of authority known as *hukmanamas* to his followers, asking them to meet at Anandpur on March 30, the day of the annual Sikh harvest festival known as *Baisakhi*.

Addressing them from the entrance of a tent that was pitched on a hill now known as *Kesgarh Sahib*, he asked who they considered him to be.

All answered: "You are our Guru." He then asked them who they were, to which they all replied: "We are your Sikhs."

He then said that he needed something from his Sikhs, to which the congregation answered: *"Hukum Karo, Sache Patshah"* (Order us, True Lord).

The Guru then drew his sword and asked for a volunteer who was willing to sacrifice his head.

No-one answered his first call, nor the second call, but on the third invitation, Daya Ram, later known as Bhai Daya Singh came forward and offered his head.

The Guru took him inside the tent and emerged shortly afterwards with blood dripping from his sword; another four volunteers followed – only for all five to later emerge from the tent unharmed.

The Guru then poured water into an iron bowl and, adding sweeteners to it, stirred it with his double-edged sword, accompanied by recitations from Sikh scripture.

This was administered to the five men who had willingly volunteered to sacrifice their lives for their Guru.

He gave them the title of *Panj Piare – The Five Beloved Ones* – and they became the first baptised Sikhs of what is known as the Khalsa.

The five were Daya Ram (Bhai Daya Singh), Dharam Das (Bhai Dharam Singh), Himmat Rai (Bhai Himmat Singh), Mohkan Chand (Bhai Mohkam Singh), and Sahib Chand (Bhai Sahib Singh).

The Guru then recited what has become the rallying cry ever since of the Khalsa: *'Waheguru ji ka Khalsa, Waheguru ji Ki Fateh'* – which means 'Khalsa belongs to God; victory belongs to God.'

It was now that he also gave them all the name of Singh ('lion'), a name that had been used since the seventh century by Rajput warriors, and designated them collectively as Khalsa – derived from a term meaning 'The Pure Ones', the body of baptised Sikhs.

The Guru then asked the five volunteers to initiate him as a member of the Khalsa, on an equal footing with them. This was done, and he became Guru Gobind Singh.

To this day members of the Khalsa regard Guru Gobind Singh as their father, and Mata Sahib Kaur, who was a member of his household, as their mother.

Women initiated into the Khalsa today are given the title of 'Kaur', indicating 'princess.'

The Guru finally addressed the assembly, telling them:

From now on, you have become casteless. No ritual, either Hindu or Muslim, will you perform nor will you believe in superstition of any kind, but only in one God who is the master and protector of all, the only creator and destroyer.

In your new order, the lowest will rank with the highest and each will be to the other a bhai (brother). No pilgrimages for you any more, nor austerities but the pure life of the household, which you should be ready to sacrifice at the call of Dharma.

Women shall be equal of men in every way. No purdah (veil) for them anymore, nor the burning alive of a widow on the pyre of her spouse (sati). He who kills his daughter, the Khalsa shall not deal with him.

He also told them of what are known as the 'Five K's' – to be observed as a sign of dedication to the Guru's ideal.

Guru Gobind Singh

These are *Kesh* – uncut hair as a representation of saintliness; *Kangha* – a comb to keep the hair clean and untangled; *Kara* – a steel bracelet to denote one universal God; *Kacchha* – an item of practical wear to denote modesty, and *Kirpan* – a steel dagger for defence.

He also told the assembly:

Smoking being an unclean and injurious habit, you will forswear. You will love the weapons of war, be excellent horsemen, marksmen and wielders of the sword, the discus and the spear.

Physical prowess will be as sacred to you as spiritual sensitivity. And, between the Hindus and Muslims, you will act as a bridge, and serve the poor without distinction of caste, colour, country or creed.

My Khalsa shall always defend the poor, and Deg (community kitchen) will be as much an essential part of your order as Teg (the sword).

And, from now onwards Sikh males will call themselves 'Singh' and women 'Kaur' and greet each other with 'Waheguruji ka Khalsa, Waheguruji ki fateh' (The Khalsa belongs to God; victory belongs to God).

Chapter three:

Lion of the Punjab

Guru Gobind Singh died at Nanded, in present day Maharashtra, on October 7, 1708, from wounds received from the blade of a Pathan assassin, and one of his last acts was to declare the holy scripture of Sikhism known as *Guru Granth Sahib* as the next permanent Sikh Guru.

His legacy survives not only through his contribution to the Sikh faith in particular, but also through the vast body of literary works he compiled in his lifetime.

This collection of his writings is known as *Dasven Padshah Da Granth* meaning *Book of the Tenth Emperor*, and is also referred to as the *Dasam Granth*.

Renowned for his devotion to the ideals of Guru Gobind Singh and of the Khalsa, Maharaja Ranjit Singh was the great nineteenth century Sikh ruler known as the *Sher-e-Punjab – Lion of the Punjab*.

Born Jevan Singh in 1789 in the Punjabi town of Gujranwala – which is now in Pakistan – his father Maha Singh was commander of the *Sukerchakia misl*, commanding a territory in western Punjab.

Succeeding his father at the age of only 12, and taking on the title of Maharaja, or Maharatta, he went on to unite all the various Sikh factions.

A skilled warrior and inspiring leader, he took the holy city of Amritsar in 1802, and over the following years fought the Afghans and drove them out of western Punjab.

He and his warriors also captured Pashtun territory, including Peshawar, and the province of Multan in southern Punjab, while other territories captured included Kashmir.

Tolerant of other religious beliefs, he allowed non-Sikhs to take part in Sikh military campaigns, and treated Hindus and Muslims equally. During his rule, he also abolished capital punishment.

One British Army officer who had known him, said: "There was no ferocity in his disposition and he never punished a criminal with death even under circumstances of aggravated offense.

"Humanity indeed, or rather tenderness for life, was a trait in the character of Ranjit Singh."

Gurudwaras, or Sikh temples erected by him

include the magnificent *Harmandir Sahib*, or Golden Temple, at Amritsar, the *Takht Sri Patna Sahib*, on the site of Guru Gobind Singh's birthplace, and the *Takht Sri Hazur Sahib*, the place of the Guru's ascension into heaven.

He died in 1839, and was later succeeded by his youngest son Dalip Singh Sukerchakia, also known as Dalip Singh, born in Lahore in 1838.

The last Maharaja of Sikh Raj, he took the throne in 1843 after a series of violent intrigues in which rival claimants to the Maharajah title and also to the legendary *Koh-i-Noor* diamond – which had originally been willed by his father to the Jagannath Temple in Orissa – killed one another.

Exiled to Britain in 1854 and later joined for a brief spell with his mother Maharani Jind Kaur, known as 'the Messalina of the Punjab' – after being dethroned and his territory annexed by the British Raj five years earlier – he became what is considered to be Britain's first Sikh settler.

It was he who rather controversially gave Queen Victoria the *Koh-i-Noor* diamond, which now forms part of the Crown Jewels, set in the crown of Queen Elizabeth II.

Kept under virtual 'house arrest' after he

was deposed and closely monitored by the British authorities, he had been persuaded to convert from the Sikh faith to Christianity one year before his exile from his native land.

Befriended by Queen Victoria and her court, he was lodged at first in London's Claridge's Hotel, before being given a house in Wimbledon, followed by another in Roehampton.

Longing for his native India, the homesick Dalip Singh said he wanted to return – but was persuaded to embark on a tour of Europe instead.

On his return to Britain in 1855 he was given an annual pension from the British government, while Castle Menzies in Perthshire, Scotland, was leased for his use.

This was followed three years later by the renting of a house at Auchlyne, also in Perthshire, and it was here that he became fondly known by the locals as 'The Black Prince of Perthshire', renowned for his shooting parties, lavish lifestyle, and love of dressing in Highland costume.

He later rented the Grantully Estate, near Aberfeldy, before returning to England in 1863 following the death of his beloved mother and taking a lease at Mulgrave Castle, in Yorkshire.

This was followed in 1863 by the purchase of the country estate of Elveden, on the borders of the counties of Suffolk and Norfolk, and where he restored the village's school, cottages and church.

Increasingly homesick, he turned his attention to studying his original faith of Sikhism and told the British authorities of his wish to return to India.

He managed to establish contact with his cousin Sardar Thakar Singh Sandhawalia and others who included the Sikh *granthi*, or priest, Pratap Singh, who travelled to England in the autumn of 1884 to meet him and reinforce his connection to the Sikh faith.

Two years later, in 1886, the British Government ruled not only against his return to India, but also against his re-conversion to Sikhism.

But, undeterred, he set sail for India in March of that year, only to be intercepted and arrested by the British authorities in Aden.

They were unable, however, to prevent his re-conversion ceremony.

Now returned to the embrace of the Sikh faith of his forefathers, Dalip Singh was forced back to Europe – eventually dying in 1893, at the age of 55, in Paris.

It had been his wish that on his death his body should be returned to India, but the British authorities refused this, fearing that the funeral of this son of the famed Lion of Punjab could cause unrest against British rule.

He was brought from Paris and buried in Elveden Church, beside the graves of his wife Maharani Bamba (Bamba Muller) and his son Prince Albert Duleep Singh.

The graves can be seen to this day, located on the west side of the church.

Dalip Singh had married twice, first to Bamba Muller and then to Ada Douglas Wetherill, and fathered a total of eight children.

They were Prince Victor Duleep Singh, Prince Frederick Duleep Singh, Prince Albert Edward Duleep Singh, Princess Bamba Sutherland, nee Singh, Princess Catherine Duleep Singh, Sophia Duleep Singh, Princess Pauline Alexandra Duleep Singh and Princess Ada Irene Beryl Duleep Singh.

All of these children died without issue, sadly ending the proud and direct line of Sikh royalty.

Chapter four:

On the world stage

From entertainment and sport to literature and politics, generations of bearers of the Singh name have gained fame and distinction through a wide range of endeavours.

Raised and educated in Glasgow, **Hardeep Singh Kohli** is the multi-talented and versatile radio and television personality and comedian whose parents first came to the United Kingdom from India in the 1960s.

Born in 1969, he is an elder brother of the equally famous **Sanjeev Singh Kohli**, the Scottish comedian, actor and writer born in 1971 and who is best known for his role as Navid Harrid in the popular BBC Scotland television comedy *Still Game* and as A.J. Jandhu in the soap *River City*.

Bearers of the Singh name have also excelled, and continue to excel, in the highly competitive world of sport – particularly on the cricket field.

Born in 1958 in Chandigarh, Punjab, Yograjsingh Bhagsingh Bhundel is the former Indian cricketer more popularly known as **Yograj Singh**.

A right-arm fast-medium bowler who played one Test and six One Day Internationals for India, he retired from first class cricket in 1985, but has since pursued a successful career as a film actor.

Best known for his role as a villain in the 1996 *Badla Jatti Da*, he has also had roles in films that include the 1980 *Chann Pardesee*, the 2001 *Sikandera*, and the 2004 *Shreeman Chanakya*.

He is the father of the Indian cricketer **Yuvraj Singh**, the left-handed batter born in 1981 in Chandigarh.

A member of the Indian cricket team since 2000, he has also captained the Indian Premier League team Kings XI Punjab.

Also on the cricket field, Vikram Raj Vir Singh is the right-arm medium-fast bowler born in 1984 in Chandigarh, and who is better known as **V.R.V. Singh**.

Considered to be one of the fastest bowlers India has produced in recent years, he has been a member of the Indian cricket team since April of 2006, making his debut in Tests against the West Indies in June of that year.

Born in 1946 in Amritsar, Punjab, **Bishan Singh Bedi** is the former left-arm bowler who captained the Indian national team in 22 Test Matches and who served for a brief period in 1990 as coach of the team.

Nicknamed 'The Turbanator' by the English-language media, **Harbhajan Singh** is the leading cricketer born in 1980 in Jalandhar, Punjab.

A son of the Punjabi businessman **Sardar Sardev Singh**, who owned a ball bearing and valve factory, the specialist bowler was awarded the Padma Shri, India's fourth highest civilian honour, in 2006.

Now pursuing careers in television commentary, film and politics, **Navjot Singh Sidhu** is the former right-handed batsman born in 1963 in Patiala, Punjab.

From cricket to golf, **Vijay Singh** is the Indo-Fijian cricketer of Hindu background who was born in 1963 in Lautoka, Fiji.

Nicknamed 'The Big Fijian', the professional golfer was number one in the official World Golf Rankings in 2004 and 2005.

The winner of three major championships – the 2000 Masters, and the PGA Championship in 1998 and 2004, he was inducted into the World Golf Hall of Fame in 2006.

In the wrestling ring, **Dara Singh Randhawa**

is the former professional Punjabi wrestler and now film actor who was born in Amritsar in 1928.

President of the wrestling body known as the All India Jat Mahasabha, his wrestling career began when he studied the Indian style of wrestling known as Pehlwani.

He competed successfully as a wrestler not only in his native land, but abroad, and began a career in Hindi films in 1962.

Throughout the 1980s and 1990s, he played the role of Hanuman in the adaptation of the Indian epic *Ramayan*, while he was inducted into the Wrestling Observer Newsletter Hall of Fame in 1996.

In field hockey, **Udham Singh** was the player born in 1928 in Sansarpur; a member of the Indian team that won gold at the 1948, 1952, and 1956 Olympics, he died in 2000.

One bearer of the Singh name who has displayed particularly astonishing sporting prowess and stamina is the Sikh marathon runner **Fauja Singh**, born in 1911 in Beas Pind, Jalandar, Punjab, and nicknamed 'The Sikh Superman'.

Having immigrated to Britain in the early 1990s and now living in Ilford, London, with his sons, at the time of writing he is the world record holder in his age bracket – with a personal best time in 2003 for the London Marathon of six hours and two minutes.

In 2004 he featured beside footballer David Beckham and former boxer Muhammad Ali in an advertising campaign for a leading international sportswear manufacturer while, speaking of running, he has said: "The first 20 miles are not difficult.

"As for the last six miles, I run while talking to God."

The recipient of a BEM (British Empire Medal), his biography, *Turbaned Tornado*, written by Khushwant Singh and who is mentioned below, was published in 2011.

Nicknamed 'The Flying Sikh', **Milkha Singh** is the former athlete who was born in Lyallpur in 1935 and who represented India in both the 1960 Olympics in Rome and the 1964 Olympics in Japan.

Winner of gold medals for the 200 and 400-metres at the 1958 Asian Games and the 1958 Commonwealth Games, he is also a recipient of the Padma Shri.

In the world of literature, **Bhai Vir Singh** was the eminent theologian, scholar and poet born in 1872 in Amritsar and who died in 1957.

A leading figure in the movement for the

revival of Punjabi literature, he was honoured with being named as 'Bhai' – indicating 'Brother of the Sikh Order.'

Referred to as 'Sixth River' of Punjab, he was given the Sahitya Award in 1955 and India's Padam Bhushan Award a year later.

Bhair Vir Singh, who launched the Khalsa Text Society in 1894, was the author of a wide range of works that include the 1953 *Mere Salan Jio*, and the 1910 *Raja Lakhdata Singh* – the first play ever written in Punjabi.

Born in Lahore in 1855, **Pratap Singh Giani** was the eminent Sikh calligraphist and scholar of Sikh scriptures who died in 1920 and who had been instrumental in the conversion back to the Sikh faith from Christianity of Dalip Singh.

In contemporary times, **Khushwant Singh** was the celebrated journalist and novelist born in 1915 in Hadali, Punjab and who died in 2014.

His books include the 1950 *The Mark of Vishnu and Other Stories*, the 1963 *Ranjit Singh: The Maharajah of the Punjab*, and the 1993 *We Indians*, while his weekly newspaper column, *With malice towards one and all*, was syndicated throughout India.

Also in contemporary times, **Simon Singh** is

the young British author, journalist and television producer who was raised in Somerset, in England, and who studied physics at Imperial College, London.

Joining the BBC's science department in 1990, he worked for a time as a producer and director and was the director of the award-winning documentary *Fermat's Last Theorem*.

His books include the 1999 *The Code Book*, while in 2001 he presented the five-part series *The Science of Secrecy* for Channel 4 television, followed four years later with *The Big Bang*.

In the world of politics, **Giani Zail Singh** was the Indian politician who was born in Punjab in 1916 and died in 1994.

A member of the Congress Party, he served from 1982 to 1987 as the 7th President of India, while earlier, from 1972 to 1977, he was Chief Minister of Punjab.

Another Singh who has played a prominent role in Indian politics is **Manmohan Singh** who served is the nation's 17th Prime Minister.

Born in 1932 in Gah, Punjub – now in the Chakual District of Pakistan – he is of a Sikh Khatri family of the Kohli clan.

A member of the National Congress Party, he

was first sworn in as the Prime Minister of India in May of 2004, becoming the first person of the Sikh faith to hold the position.

An economist by profession, he has also held the post of Union Minister for Finance, while from 1991 to 1996 of Finance Minister and has previously worked for organisations that included the International Monetary Fund and the United Nations.

In the kitchen, **Tony Singh** is the celebrity chef of Scottish-Sikh roots born in Leith, near Edinburgh.

A member of prestigious bodies that include the Master Chefs of Great Britain, the Craft Guild of Chefs and the Scottish Chefs Association, television shows in which he has featured include *Great British Menu*, while in 2015 he explored the culinary delights of the Punjab.

Working in the restaurant business in his native Scotland, running enterprises that have included *Tony's Table*, in Edinburgh, his many accolades include a Scottish Chefs Award.